The Middle Ages

An illustrated introduction to the impact of the Normans on Europe and the British Isles, with special reference to Ireland.

Kathleen Gormley
Sheila Johnston

Illustrated by John Brogan

COLOURPOINT

8   7   6   5   4   3   2   1

ISBN 1 898392 21 8

Layout and design: Sheila Johnston
Typeset by: Colourpoint Books
Printed by: ColourBooks

Colourpoint Books
Unit D5, Ards Business Centre
Jubilee Road
NEWTOWNARDS
Co Down
BT23 4YH

Tel: 01247 820505 (direct)
  or 01247 819787 ext 239
Fax: 01247 821900

The Authors
Kathleen Gormley teaches History and Politics at St. Cecilia's College, Derry. She has a B.A. (Hons) in History and a Masters in Modern History from the University of Ulster at Coleraine. From 1993 -1995 she was seconded to the Western Education and Library Board as a History Advisory Teacher. She is past-president of the North-West Archaeological and Historical Society, past vice-chairman of the Federation for Ulster Local Studies, a member of the Historic Monuments Council for Northern Ireland and committee member of the North West branch of the Historical Association. She is author of several local history publications and has worked on a variety of educational publications.

Sheila Johnston is a graduate of Queen's University, Belfast. She was College Librarian in Fermanagh College and then manager of the Study Centre in Omagh College, Co Tyrone, until 1994. She has published many short stories and articles as well as contributing to several local radio programmes. Past winner of the the Omagh District Council Creative Writing Prize. She has written a biography, and co-produced a documentary for Radio Ulster, on Alice Milligan, and edited a book of her poems. She is now a full time publisher and writer.

Acknowledgments
Norman Johnston: 4, 9, 21 (top), 39 (ruins, plan), 40, 44 (King John), 48, 54 (cross), 55, 56 (left), 57, 58.
Sheila Johnston: 7, 47
James Davis: 5 (William, Harold, king), 8 (all), 18, 22 (spiral), 43 (bishop), 45 (Black Death graphic), 48 (monk)
© Crown copyright, reproduced with the permission of the Controller of Her Majesty's Stationery Office: 20, 22 (keep), 39 (reconstruction), 56 (reconstruction)
Kindly supplied by the Geraldine Tralee Exhibition, Tralee, Co Kerry   36
Hulton Getty Picture Library: 44
National Gallery of Ireland: 52
All reproductions from the Bayeux Tapestry are by special permission of the City of Bayeux.

The short play on pages 50 and 51 is adapted from *The Living Past 3*, by Tim McGillicuddy, published in 1973 by The Educational Company of Ireland, Ltd.

Contents

Welcome to the Middle Ages! 4

The Norman Conquest 5

1 Who were the Normans? 6
2 Where did they come from? 7
3 The fight for the English throne 8
4 Rivals do battle 9
5 Saxon soldiers 10
6 Norman soldiers 11
7 The story told by the Bayeux Tapestry 12
8 Two accounts of the Battle of Hastings 14
9 How did Harold die? 16
10 Taking control 17
11 The Feudal System 18
12 The Domesday Book 19
13 Castles 20
14 Stone castles 22
15 Castles under attack 23

Medieval Society 24

16 How a Norman person was named 25
17 Norman food 26
18 Norman clothes 28

19 Norman games and pastimes 30
20 Norman justice 32
21 The poor 34
22 The rich 35
23 Town life 36
24 Country life 37
25 Convents and monasteries 39
26 Holy men 40
27 Holy women 41
28 Women in medieval times 42
29 Getting married 43
30 Disease and death 44
31 The Black Death 45
32 Knights and Crusades 46

Ireland and the Normans 47

33 Ireland before the Normans 48
34 Dermot MacMurrough 49
35 Dermot and the Normans 50
36 A wedding in Waterford 52
37 Why the Normans came 53
38 The Normans invade 54
39 The conquest of Ulster 55
40 De Courcy: the Norman who wanted to be king 56
41 De Courcy's legacy lives on 57
42 Carrickfergus Castle 58
43 Carrickfergus Castle — the siege 59
44 Carrickfergus Castle — change over time 60
45 Norman soldiers and Irish soldiers 62
46 The Greencastle skeleton 63
Timeline 64

Welcome to the Middle Ages!

Nowadays, when we talk about 'middle age' we are probably talking about the age people are when they are not young any more, but they can't be described as old just yet. They are not at the beginning or near the end on their lives, so we say they are *middle aged*.

We can think about history a bit like this. There was a time at the beginning of history and there is the time we live in ourselves. The events described in this book didn't take place near the beginning of history, but they weren't near our time either. They took place about the middle of history.

So we call this time the **Middle Ages**. Sometimes it is also called the **Medieval period**.

Jousting was a favourite pastime for knights in the Middle Ages. Two knights wearing armour would ride at each other holding long, pointed lances. Each one would try to knock the other off his horse. The lances weren't very sharp so that they didn't do any real harm. A joust was a great day out for everyone. The joust in the picture was staged at Littlecote Manor in Berkshire, England.

The Norman Conquest

The next few pages tell the story of how the Normans invaded and took over Britain. This page will give you some idea of what you are going to learn about.

Before the Normans came, the people who ruled England were called **Saxons**.

1. Some Normans decide to leave France and go with their Duke, William, of Normandy to conquer England.

2. The Normans arrive in England and go to battle with Harold, King of England, at Hastings. They win and William becomes king.

3. William and the Normans build many castles across the land to make sure he has control.

4. William makes people swear their loyalty to him and pay him taxes.

5. He organises society into a feudal system, where the king owns all the land and shares it with his loyal subjects.

6. The Normans go on to invade Scotland, Wales and Ireland.

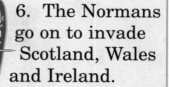

1. Who were the Normans?

The Normans were descendants of the Vikings. They came to France in the tenth century.

They were called 'Northmen' because they came from the north, from countries like Norway and Denmark.

Some of these Vikings probably raided France as pirates and many of them stayed on the land they invaded.

?

1 Why were the first Normans called Northmen?

2 Can you think of reasons why they left their homes in the north?

Key Words: Viking, invaded, descendants.

2. Where did they come from?

The Normans settled in the north of France. The French king gave them land in an area called **Normandy**.

In return for the land which the French king had given them, they provided an army of soldiers for the many wars which were taking place across Europe at this time.

The Normans soon took on the French way of life. They began to speak French and soon called themselves 'Frenchmen', not Normans. They also became Christians and built many churches.

The Normans were very good soldiers. They also conquered new lands for themselves.

The leader of the Normans from 1035 was **William, Duke of Normandy**. He was later to become King of England.

Key Words: **conquered, Europe.**

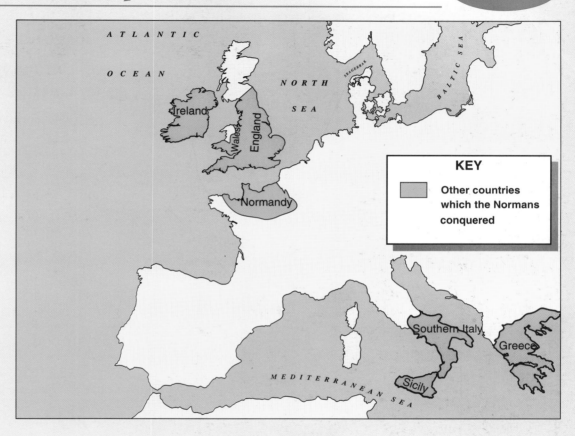

KEY

Other countries which the Normans conquered

?

1 Why did the King of France give the Normans land of their own?

2 What other countries did the Normans invade?

3. The fight for the English throne

When Edward, King of England, died he had no **heirs**. There were three people who all thought they should be the new king. Read about them and see who you think should be king.

?

Which rival ...

(a)... was English;

(b)...had the support of the Pope;

(c)...was named by Edward;

(d)...was crowned by the King's Council;

(e)...had relatives who once ruled England?

Harold, Earl of Godwin

... had been named as the next king by Edward, the king who had just died.

... was Edward's brother-in-law.

... was an Englishman.

... was crowned by the King's Council when Edward died.

William, Duke of Normandy

... said that Harold had promised him the throne after he saved Harold from being shipwrecked.

... was a Norman from France.

... was a good soldier and ruler.

... had the support of the Pope.

Harald Hardrada, King of Norway

... was a Viking from Norway.

... had relatives who had once ruled England.

... was supported by Harold's brother.

... was a powerful soldier.

4. Rivals do battle

Edward, King of England, died on 5th January 1066. The King's Council crowned Harold Godwin as the next king.

On 18th September 1066, Harald Hardrada invaded the north of England. King Harold took his Saxon army to Stamford Bridge near York and fought Harald Hardrada's army. Harold won on 25th September 1066.

On 1st October news was brought to Harold that William of Normandy had landed at Pevensey on the south coast of England three days earlier. Harold and his Saxon army had to make the long journey south to meet William and his army. This march took ten days.

Meanwhile, the Normans were able to wait and rest.

1   Which army do you think was most ready to fight on 14th October 1066? Why?

2   On one side of a page, write out all the dates which are mentioned on this page. Beside each date say what happened on that day.

3   What happened on 28th September 1066?

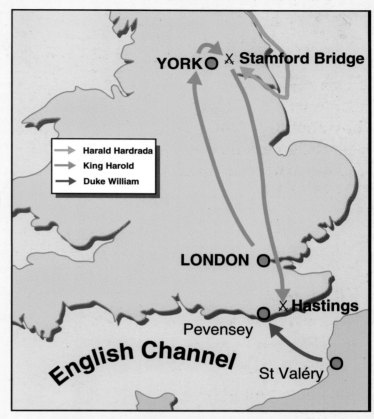

This map shows the journeys the three rivals took in 1066.

Harold arrived at Senlac Hill near Hastings on Saturday 14th October **1066**. Between 9.00 am and dusk, the **Battle of Hastings** took place.

5. Saxon soldiers

Both Harold and William had well trained armies. Harold's soldiers were fighting on their own land, but William's soldiers were well used to fighting in foreign countries. Each army had about 7,000 men.

Saxon soldiers

- Harold had some well trained soldiers who travelled on horseback.

- They fought on foot with two handed battle-axes and spears.

- They carried shields.

- Some also had swords.

- They were known as housecarls.

- Ordinary soldiers had less equipment and were not as well trained and would not have had horses.

Key Word: housecarls.

10

6. *Norman soldiers*

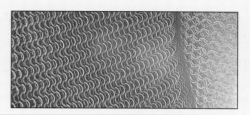

This is a close-up of a piece of chain mail

Norman soldiers

- Norman knights fought on horseback and were dressed in chain mail.

- Chain mail was made by joining hundreds of metal rings together.

- They wore helmets and carried swords, spears and kite-shaped shields.

- William also had foot soldiers and archers. The archers could kill a man wearing armour from 50 metres away. If the man was not wearing any armour an archer could kill him from 100 metres away.

Key Words: chain mail.

11

7. The story told by the Bayeux Tapestry

The Bayeux Tapestry is a piece of embroidered linen, made by the Normans, which tells the story of how the Normans invaded England. It is 70 metres long and 50 cms wide. It was sewn using blue, green, red and yellow thread. It has 72 panels.

Some of the panels are shown on these two pages to tell the Norman side of the story.

1. Edward, King of England, sends Harold to Normandy to tell William that he has chosen William to be the next king of England.

2. On the way, Harold is shipwrecked and taken prisoner. William gives orders for him to be released.

3. William makes Harold swear an oath of loyalty, on holy relics, that he will support William as the next king of England.

4. In England, King Edward dies.

Key Words: tapestry, panels, oath, council.

5. Harold forgets about the oath and is crowned King of England.

6. William is told that Harold has been crowned king. He is angry and invades England. He lands in Sussex with an army of 5000 men.

7. The two armies meet on a hill near Hastings and fight a fierce battle.

?

1 Divide your class into 8 groups. Each group draw one of the scenes from the Bayeux Tapestry. Using your pictures, tell the story in your own words.

2 Would the Saxons tell the story differently?

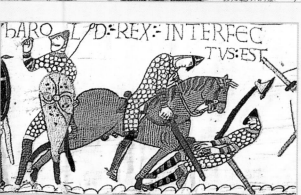

8. Harold is killed with an arrow and his army runs away.

8. Two accounts of the Battle of Hastings

If two people in your class told the story of your first day at school, the two stories would probably be very different.

So historians studying the past have to be very careful to look at as many different accounts of the same event as they can. This way they have a clearer picture of what really happened.

The two accounts on the next page tell part of the story of the Battle of Hastings.

William de Poitiers was a Norman.

The Anglo-Saxon Chronicles were written by Saxon monks.

A. What the Anglo-Saxon Chronicle said

"William attacked Harold by surprise, but Harold fought hard. There were a lot of men killed on both sides. The Normans got control of the battlefield. It was as if God was on their side because of the sins of the people.

William waited for them to surrender but they didn't and then his troops ravaged everywhere."

B. What William de Poitiers said

"At last the Saxons began to tire. Evening was falling and they saw that they could not hold out much longer against the Normans. They had lost a big number of soldiers and their king Harold and his two brothers were dead.

The number of Norman soldiers had not dropped and they fought with the same strength as they had at the beginning of the battle.

The Saxons ran away, some on horseback and some on foot. The Normans followed them, bringing a happy end to the battle."

Key Words: ravaged, chronicle.

?

1 Which of the accounts on this page agree with each of these statements:

   Many Saxons died.

   Both Normans and Saxons died.

   Few Normans were killed.

   The Saxons ran away.

   William was cruel.

   Harold fought hard.

2 Which account was for the Normans? Which account was for the Saxons? Why do you think this?

3 Now write what you think is a correct account of the battle.

4 Why do you think accounts of the past differ?

9. *How did Harold die?*

Some people think *this* was Harold and that he was killed by an arrow in his eye.

Some people think one of these soldiers was Harold and that he was killed with a sword.

Sometimes, after someone dies there is a lot of talk about how it happened. This is what happened after the death of Harold, King of England.

One account, written by an Anglo-Saxon monk, says that Harold was killed by an arrow in his eye. Another account written by a famous Norman, says that Harold survived long after the battle, and lived in a monastery.

1 List the different things that might have happened to Harold at Hastings.

2 Do any of the stories agree?

3 Using a computer, write a newspaper account of Harold's death the way *you* think it happened. Copy the picture on this page onto your newspaper page and label it to support your story.

16

10. Taking control

William won the Battle of Hastings on 14th October 1066, but that did not mean that everyone accepted him as the new King of England. He had to take control of the country. The panels on this page tell you how he did it.

 1. After the Battle of Hastings William marched towards London. On the way he destroyed many towns and castles. This made people realise that he would deal harshly with his enemies.

 2. William built many castles throughout the countryside to provide strongholds for his followers and supporters. Sometimes the Normans built castles just to show off their great wealth.

  **5.** In order to run his country and keep a large army William needed money. He set up a system of recording the details of his subjects and what they owned. This meant he could work out what to tax them. The document recording all these details is called the **Domesday Book**.

 4. He took away the lands of the Saxon lords who had fought against him at Hastings. Others had to swear an oath of loyalty to him as king.

William was crowned King of England on **Christmas Day 1066**, in the new church of Westminster in London. Edward had built it and he based its design on a church in Normandy.

 **3.** He reorganised the system of owning land. This was called the **feudal system**.

11. *The Feudal System*

The **feudal system** was how society was organised in the Middle Ages.

It was based mostly on land and who owned the land. The Normans introduced this system to England.

The king owned all the land, but because he could not control or farm it all himself he gave some to his **barons**. In return for this land they promised to be loyal to William and train **knights** for his army.

The barons gave some of this land to their knights in return for their loyalty and their promise to fight.

The knights gave some of their land to the **villeins** who had to work for the knight for some days each year, and had to pay him taxes.

Villeins were peasants and they were thought of as the least important people in society.

I am the king. I own all the land. I rule because I am strong.

We are the barons. The king gives us land and we swear loyalty to him. We also send money, or men to fight for him if he needs them.

We are knights. The baron gives us land and we swear to be loyal to him and to fight for him sometimes.

We are the villeins. The knights give us land and we farm it to feed our families. We have to work for the knight some days in the year and we have to pay him taxes.

12. The Domesday Book

The **Domesday Book** was the record of a survey which William the Conqueror had carried out in **1086**.

It was a written record of all that his subjects owned. It listed all the estates in the land.

The survey was carried out by a group of people who went from county to county asking people questions about what they owned.

The decisions made were written in the Domesday Book and could not be changed.

People had to swear an oath that they were telling the truth about their property.

This book was very important for the king but it has also become very important for historians because it tells so much about England in 1086.

?

1. Why do you think the king made the people swear an oath?

2. Why do you think the soldier has a sword in his hand?

Key Words: oath, historians.

13. Castles

A motte and bailey castle

The Keep

This was the tower on top of the motte. It was a lookout and a strong place to fight from.

Wooden bridge

This joined the keep to the bailey. If there was a battle, the soldiers in the castle could smash this bridge and fight from the keep on the motte.

The Moat

This was the ditch round the whole castle. Sometimes, but not always, it was filled with water.

The Motte

This was a small hill made by digging a circular ditch and piling the soil in the middle.

The Bailey

This was a courtyard surrounded by a fence or palisade. It was at a lower level than the motte. The soldiers lived and slept here.

The first castles built by the Normans were not built as great symbols of their power or wealth.

They were built to provide a strong place to protect the Normans from the native people who were not always friendly.

20

The Normans needed to build their first castles fast so they used materials from the countryside around them. They often used hills — or mounds — that were already there and built **motte and bailey** castles on top of them.

Clough Castle, near Downpatrick, as it is today. The bailey is the lower hill on the right. Can you point to the motte?

This is a panel from the Bayeux Tapestry. It shows William's men building a castle at Hastings. They are heaping up earth on their shovels to make the motte higher.

?

1 What materials do you think would be needed to build a motte and bailey castle?

2 As you can see from the picture of Clough Castle above, very little is left of motte and bailey castles today. What is missing? Why do you think this is?

3 Imagine you are actually watching William's men building the castle at Hastings. Tell what you see in your own words. Think of words like: **layers**, **shovels**, **mound**, **hard work**, **tired**, **overseer**.

21

14. Stone castles

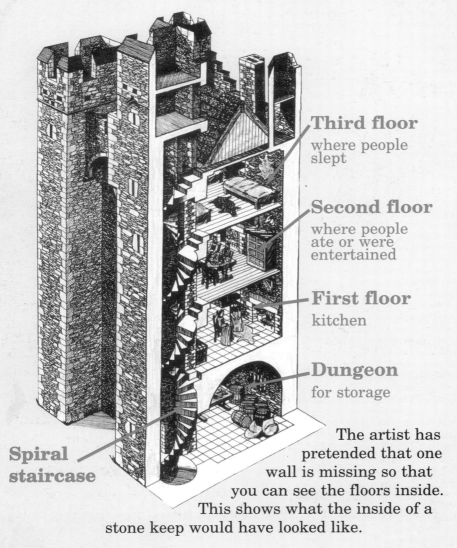

Third floor
where people slept

Second floor
where people ate or were entertained

First floor
kitchen

Dungeon
for storage

Spiral staircase

The artist has pretended that one wall is missing so that you can see the floors inside. This shows what the inside of a stone keep would have looked like.

After the Normans took control of the countryside, they replaced some of their motte and bailey castles with large stone castles. Sometimes they used the site of the motte and bailey castle. The wooden keep was replaced with a stone one. Later, an outer wall was added.

These castles were much bigger and took longer to build than their first castles. They were better protected and sometimes they were surrounded by a moat which meant that the castle could be cut off by water.

These castles were also homes for the wealthy barons who would have feasts in the **Great Hall** of the castle.

Spiral staircases were built into the walls at corners to save space.

15. Castles under attack

!

1 Match the following words to the right meanings:

Ballista: long ladders used to climb the castle walls

Scaling ladders: pounded the walls or gates of the castle

Catapults: large crossbows which fired arrows

Battering rams: used to fire stones over the walls

2 Using matchboxes, plasticine, lollipop sticks and rubber bands, make models of the weapons to attack a castle.

In Norman times there were no big cannon to attack stone castles, but gradually weapons which could attack them were invented. The attackers used **battering rams** which pounded the walls of the castle. They also had huge crossbows, called **ballistas**, to fire large arrows.

If the attackers still couldn't get the castle owner to surrender, then their army would surround the castle and stop those inside getting any food supplies in. They tried to starve them into giving up. This is called a **siege**. Sieges didn't always work, because castles usually had a well for water inside, and they could store a large supply of food.

Medieval society

The next section is about what it was like to be an ordinary person in Norman times. This page tells you of some of the things you will learn about.

Most people lived in the country and worked on the land.

Houses were small and dirty. They were mostly built from wood, there was a great risk of fire.

The Normans were Christians and built many churches and monasteries.

Norman clothes and pastimes were very different to ours.

Some methods of Norman justice were so advanced that they are still used today. Others were not so good.

There were many diseases and plagues when thousands of people died. One of the most famous was called the **Black Death**.

There was a great difference between the lives of the rich and poor.

Women were not treated as equal in Norman times. Many were considered to be the property of their husbands.

16. How a Norman person was named

Our surnames are usually handed down from one generation to the next, but in Norman times ordinary people would just have had one name. There might be a lot of people called Edgar or John in one place, so to tell them apart, they were sometimes given an extra name.

People could be named after their father, local places, jobs, and even given a nickname.

If you were named after your father you might be called 'son of William' or 'son of John'.

If you were named after a local place, you might be called 'Grove' or 'Woods'.

If you were called after your job you might be called 'Cook' or 'Thatcher'.

If you came from somewhere else, you might be called after the place you came from, such as 'Kent' or 'Fleming' (from Flanders).

You might be given a nickname to describe you, such as 'Short' or 'Redhead'.

Hey! did you hear that John has married Matilda?

Do you mean John the Butcher?

No, John the Redhead.

Donald's son, Edgar, won't like that.

Why not?

Edgar told me last week that *he* wanted to marry Matilda.

No, no, it's Matilda, the daughter of that new man from York, that *he* has a notion of.

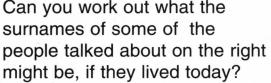

?

1 Can you work out what the surnames of some of the people talked about on the right might be, if they lived today?

2 In pairs, make up a similar conversation to this one.

17. Norman food

Rich people and poor people ate very different sorts of food.

The poor would have eaten vegetables, cheese, oatmeal porridge and dark bread which was baked in the oven of the Lord of the Manor.

Meat wasn't often eaten by the poor. Most meat was roasted on a spit or boiled.

Sometimes people poached rabbits or deer from the king's forest. Poachers were brought before the Lord of the Manor for judgement. Here is one poacher's tale:

Sir, for pity's sake do not blame me. I went the other evening to the pond and I looked at the fish which were playing in the water. They were so beautiful. I caught one and brought it home.

My dear wife has been sick for a month and she hasn't been eating but said she would like to eat a fish. So I brought her one.

Key Word: poacher.

!

Divide the class into groups of four.

Each person in a group pretend to be one of these people:

The poacher

The Lord of the Manor

The poacher's wife

A neighbour

Now act out the story of the poacher.

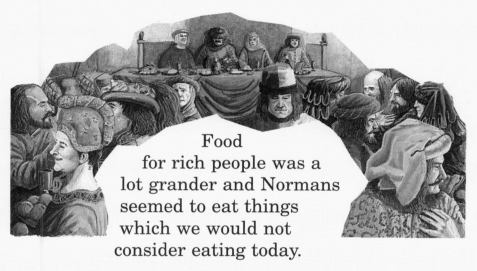

Food for rich people was a lot grander and Normans seemed to eat things which we would not consider eating today.

Feasts could go on for hours and people ate and drank a lot. Guests were warned not to eat and drink so much that they could not get up from the table! To overeat like this is called **gluttony**.

Where people sat at a feast or banquet depended on how important they were. Important people sat at the best tables. Less important people were given the worst seats and had to share bowls of food.

Menu for a Feast

Larded boar's head
Duck, pheasant
Chicken stuffed with
egg yolks, currants
and cinnamon
Meat soup
Rabbits, hares
Birds
Cheese pie
Wine and bread

! 1 Rule a page into two halves. On one side write down the food from this menu which you would eat today. On the other side write down food that you would not eat today.

2 Now design a menu for a feast today.

Key Words: gluttony, banquet.

During the Middle Ages there were many changes in the way rich people dressed.

Crusaders coming back from the Holy Land would have brought **silk** in many colours. Sometimes cloth had gold thread.

This was too expensive for poor people and they used local material to make their cloth. Flax was made into **linen** and they spun their own **woollen** cloth.

Women's **dresses** were very long and it became fashionable for them to trail the floor. **Cloaks** were worn over dresses. Around their waist was a **girdle** or belt.

Women may have worn veils over their heads like nuns. These were called **wimples**. Later on in the Middle Ages women put their plaits in gold net bags and some women wore very grand head-dresses.

Men wore long **tunics**. Outdoors, they wore **cloaks** over these. These were trimmed with fur and were often fastened with a **brooch**.

Because a lot of rich men went hawking for sport, **gloves** became fashionable.

Shoes were pointed, and became more pointed as time went on. The long toes were stuffed with horse hair.

?

Do you think the pictures on these two pages show rich people or poor people? Why do you think this?

Draw a Norman man and a Norman woman.

Now label all the items of clothing that are mentioned on these two pages.

19. Norman games and pastimes

Norman games were different from games we would play today. The pictures on these two pages show some of their favourite pastimes.

Juggling

Juggling was a great skill and would have been watched for amusement.

 **Playing chess or draughts**

This was a game which women and men could join in equally.

Playing the harp

This was a favourite instrument.

Dancing
Dancing did not take as much energy as it does today!

Another game which the Normans played was called 'hoodsman blind'. Sometimes we play this today. Can you guess what *we* call it?

Draw two Norman people playing a game of hoodsman blind. Remember to give them Norman clothes!

Acrobats
Groups of performing acrobats would travel from one castle to the next.

20. Norman justice

What happened if people did something wrong in Norman times? Punishment may seem hard compared to nowadays.

Trial by Combat

The Normans believed that God was on the side of the innocent. If there was a quarrel between two noblemen, they were asked to fight each other. If no-one won, then the person who had blamed the other for a crime was called a liar. He could be asked to give up his lands, or flee the country or pay a fine.

?

1 Study both of these pages. Which of these punishments would *not* be used today? Why not?

2 Which of these punishments would still be used today?

Trial by Ordeal

This punishment was for less important people. They were asked to do something very difficult, such as walking twelve steps holding a hot piece of iron in their hands, or putting their hands into boiling water. The burnt hands were bandaged and if the wound healed people said the man was innocent, and if it didn't heal he was guilty.

The ducking stool

The ducking stool was often used as a punishment for women who nagged or gossiped. Women were tied to a chair and lowered into the water again and again.

Trial by Jury

This method of Norman justice is still used today. A person accused of a crime was judged by twelve men of the same social standing as himself.

21. The poor

Peasants were at the very bottom of the social system. They lived in houses of one room made from wood, or from stone if it was available locally.

The roof was made of thatch. One corner of the room was used to keep animals in. The heat from the animals helped to keep the house warm. There wasn't very much furniture and people slept on straw.

Peasants worked for the Lord of the Manor. Some of them were given some land which they could farm for themselves. In return for this land they worked for the Lord of the Manor on a number of days each year.

Other peasants had no land and worked for food or money.

22. The rich

Rich people lived in castles or manor houses. These were made of stone. As well as the lord and his family there might be as many as 50 servants.

Kitchens were large, busy buildings. Lines of servants carried the dishes into the Great Hall for dinner. Before the Lord of the Manor ate his food, it was tasted by someone else in case it had been poisoned.

Make two columns. At the top of one write 'Rich' and at the top of the other write 'Poor'. Put these statements below the correct heading:

Houses with one room

Worked for the Lord of the Manor

Large kitchens

Thatched roof

Many servants

Slept on straw

Collected taxes

Food was tasted

The picture above shows a banquet going on in the Great Hall of Carrickfergus Castle.

The Great Hall was also used for the Lord of the Manor to hold his court (when he gave out judgements in disputes) and was where he collected the local taxes.

23. Town life

Most people in the Middle Ages worked on the land, but small towns grew up around castles where people gathered to trade. The number of people in Britain increased. In 1086 there were 2 million people but by 1300 there were 7 million.

Most homes were small and made of wood. Wealthy merchants had two storey houses.

Streets were muddy because people threw their rubbish into the open drains. There were no bathrooms. Kitchens were sometimes put in the yard because of the danger of setting fire to the wooden houses. A **curfew bell** was sounded every night, and when people heard it they had to put out their fires.

This man is a leather worker. Do you know what the man in the other picture is? What might he have bought from the leather worker?

Even though it was a town, many people kept

chickens or pigs in the yard beside the houses.

Many craftsmen lived in towns and most towns held **markets** where country people could come and sell vegetables and cheese, and buy things like furniture and candles.

Big markets were called **fairs** and could last up to three weeks. At these fairs there would be entertainers like minstrels, jugglers, sword-swallowers and clowns.

24. *Country life*

Life was hard for people in the country. They would have to get up early and work all day in the fields.

The man in the picture above is sowing his wheat. Then he has to reap and winnow it.

? Do you know in what seasons the farmer in these three pictures would have carried out these tasks?

Oxen were used to pull carts. Very often, two were yoked together.

Key Words: oxen, yoked, reap, winnow.

37

Now say what you think the people in the pictures on this page are doing.

Poor people had to grow their own food and make their own clothes. There were no shops such as we have today.

?

1 What two jobs had to be done in order to make clothes?

2 Why do you think some animals were killed before the winter?

3 Why do you think other animals were fed during the winter?

25. Convents and monasteries

Kings and nobles paid monks and nuns to pray for them. They hoped that these prayers would save their souls and that they would go to heaven.

The Normans were very famous for setting up **convents** and **monasteries**. Nuns lived in convents and monks lived in monasteries. They thought of themselves as God's warriors and so, when they invaded and took over lands, they built monasteries and churches so that people would be encouraged to become Christians.

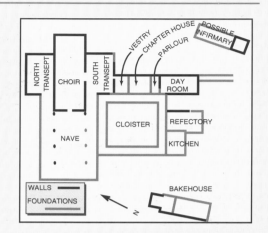

This picture shows what remains of Inch Abbey in Co Down.

The diagram above is a plan of the rooms in Inch Abbey.

The **church** is the cross-shaped part on the left, made up of the transepts, choir and nave.

The **cloister** was where the monks sat or walked about to relax or meditate.

Items needed for church services were kept in the **vestry**. A chapter of the rules was read every day in the **chapter house**.

Monks could talk in the **parlour**, and the **dayroom** was for indoor activities. The **infirmary** was the hospital and the monks ate in the **refectory**.

26. Holy men

Many new religious orders for men were founded in the Middle Ages for those who wanted to give their lives to serving God.

One order was founded by Saint Benedict and these monks were called **Benedictines**. Saint Benedict said monks should obey three main rules. You can read them in the box on this page.

Monks were to spend their time working and praying. They grew their own vegetables and kept animals as well as making their own butter, bread and beer.

Not all monks led holy lives. Some were blamed for eating and drinking too much.

The three main rules of St Benedict	
Chastity	— never get married
Poverty	— have no money
Obedience	— do as they were told by the head of the monastery

?

Which vows have been broken by the monk described by Chaucer ?

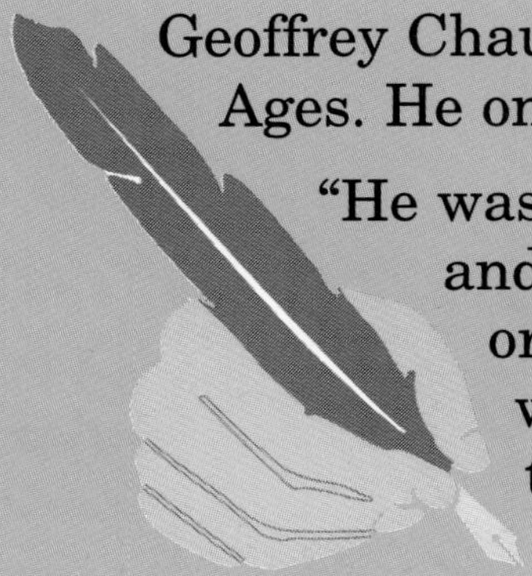

Geoffrey Chaucer was a writer in the Middle Ages. He once described a monk like this:

"He was a powerful man who loved riding and hunting. He would not obey orders and waste his time working with his hands. His sleeves were trimmed with grey fur."

27. Holy women

Many women became nuns in the Middle Ages. Some queens and princesses became nuns. They thought this would protect their families and their kingdoms.

Nuns lived in convents. Many of the nuns were rich women and many of them were allowed to wear their own clothes.

?

1 Read Chaucer's description of the nun. What three pieces of jewellery did the nun wear?

2 Draw a picture of this nun and label her jewellery.

3 How different is this nun from the one in the picture?

A famous story by Geoffrey Chaucer described the head of a convent like this:

"Her cloak, I noticed, had a graceful charm;

She wore a coral trinket on her arm:

A set of beads, the gaudiest tricked in green,

Whence a gold brooch of the brightest green"

Not all nuns were like the one Geoffrey Chaucer described. Many led very religious lives. The Franciscan nuns were called 'Poor Clares' after their founder, St Clare. This order still exists today.

28. Women in medieval times

Women were not treated as equal to men. They had little choice about who they married, or even *if* they married. The king had the right to make the widows and daughters of barons marry for money. Barons could deal with their tenants in the same way.

Before the Normans invaded Britain, women could own land just as men could. They could leave this land to whoever they liked when they died. From 1066, this changed and a woman's land was hers only until she married.

Many Normans married Anglo-Saxon women.

These marriages between Saxons and Normans helped the Norman and Saxon people to live more peacefully together.

This also meant that English as a language did not die out because Saxon mothers, who spoke English, taught it to their children, rather than French which was spoken by their fathers.

The writer of a twelfth century book said:

A woman is completely in the power of her husband. Everything she has is his.

!

Read the following statements about Norman women and say if they are right or not.

1 The role of women changed for the worse when the Normans came.

2 Women were not equal to their husbands.

3 Marriages between Normans and Saxons were a good thing.

29. *Getting married*

The clergy liked people to get married in church but many people didn't have a proper wedding ceremony.

When two people got engaged they made a **hand-fast**. This could be followed by a blessing at the church door.

As time went on the church became stricter about marriage and preached that marriage should last for ever.

One bishop said:

> You must keep your wife whether you like it or not, even if she is a cross-patch who drinks, swears and eats too much.

!

1   Look at the picture of the wedding in the Middle Ages and say how different a wedding today would be.

2   Find out what promises married couples make to each other today during their wedding ceremony.

30. Disease and death

In the Middle Ages people believed that a bird called a Calandrus could tell you if a sick person would recover. If it turned its head towards the sick person, he would recover. If it turned its head away, the person would die.

I'm sure you have realised by now that people in Norman times did not have a very healthy way of life. Even rich people did not have baths very often. Toilets in castles were called **latrines**. They were usually in the corner of a tower. The waste from them ran into the moat outside. In hot weather, people sometimes had to move out of their castles altogether, because of the smell!

Doctors were not very sure how people caught diseases. Many believed in **astrology**. They thought the positions of the stars affected how people felt. Others believed you could tell how healthy someone was by looking at their urine.

Blood-letting was a popular cure for a lot of sicknesses. Doctors would cut a person's arm and make them bleed. They hoped that 'bad blood' was being let out.

Ordinary people used charms and herbs. There was usually a wise woman in the village to help with childbirth.

Kings and queens were supposed to have power over illness. They would sometimes touch sick people who believed they would get better.

There was no anaesthetic and so there weren't many operations. It would have been much too painful. The local barber would carry out any small operations.

Here is a model of King John sitting on a toilet in Carrickfergus Castle!

31. *The Black Death*

What were the symptoms?

In 1348 a terrible disease swept across Europe and came to Britain. It was carried by fleas on black rats. One third of the population died.

By 1349 it had reached Ireland, Scotland and Wales.

Boils the size of an egg

Coughing up blood

Red and black spots on the skin

Doctors did not know what caused it and thought that it had something to do with bad air.

Others thought that it was a punishment from God for a bad life.

People called it **the plague** or the **Black Death**.

THE BLACK DEATH

It was discovered that the Black Death was carried into the country in the cargo holds of ships.

Ships were made to wait out in the harbour until they were fumigated.

Plagues did happen again but none were as bad as this.

Key Words: pest house, fumigated, symptoms.

What people thought they could do about the Black Death.

1 Try not to breathe in toilet smells.
2 Houses where someone had the plague should be marked with a red cross.
3 Pray to God to stop his anger.
4 Build special pest houses outside the town.
5 Cover windows.
6 Carry sweet smelling herbs or flowers.
7 Do nothing and hope for the best.

45

32. Knights and Crusades

The Middle Ages was really the 'Age of Knights'. Knights had a code of chivalry which said that they should be brave and courteous and generous as well as fighting well in battle. Many medieval stories tell of knights saving people from danger.

Knights were often involved in battle. Many of these battles took place during the great **Crusades** of the time.

The word 'crusade' comes from the Latin word meaning 'cross'.

At the end of the eleventh century, the Pope asked for help to re-capture Jerusalem from the Turks and other places where Christians might want to go on pilgrimages. These knights wore the cross of Jesus on their armour. They captured Jerusalem and other places.

This meant that people could safely visit these lands.

Key Word: Crusades.

?

1 Why do you think many knights wore crosses?

2 Find out why Christians would want to go on a pilgrimage to Jerusalem.

Ireland and the Normans

Now we are going to look at what happened in Ireland, both before and after the Normans came. This page tells you some of the things you will learn about.

1. Before the Normans came, Ireland was divided into small kingdoms, each with its own king. There were five main towns which had been set up by Vikings who had invaded earlier.

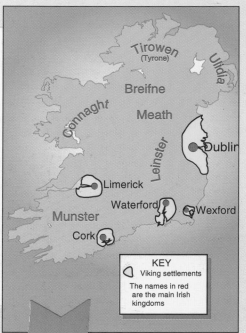

KEY
◁ Viking settlements
The names in red are the main Irish kingdoms

Tirowen (Tyrone)
Ulidia
Breifne
Connaght
Meath
Leinster
Dublin
Limerick
Waterford
Wexford
Munster
Cork

4. Other Normans heard that there was land to be conquered in Ireland and more came over and brought their families to live there.

3. The Normans agreed to help him. They landed in Ireland. After many battles they built castles and took control of large parts of Ireland.

2. Some of the Irish kings fought each other. One of them, Dermot MacMurrough, went to the King of England, who was a Norman, for help.

47

Most Irish people were descended from the Celts and Vikings who had invaded Ireland before this time.

The only towns in Ireland were the Viking trading towns of Dublin, Wexford, Waterford, Limerick and Cork.

Ireland was divided into a number of kingdoms. Each kingdom was ruled by a different king. The **High King**, or **Ard Rí**, as he was known, was the most powerful of all the kings. The other kings were expected to support him in battle and to give him grain and cattle.

Most people made their living by raising cattle and there were many cattle raids and battles between the small kingdoms.

There were many monasteries in Ireland.

The picture above shows a reconstruction of a Celtic monastery at the Ulster History Park, near Omagh, Co Tyrone. The tall round tower was used as a store and for taking shelter if the Vikings attacked.

Be thou my soul's shelter, be thou my strong tower;
O raise thou me heavenward, great Power of my power.
High King of Heaven, thou heaven's bright sun,
O grant me its joys after victory is won.

Key Words: **High King, reconstruction.**

?

Read the lines from the ancient hymn on the left. What parts of it tell you that it was written by an Irish person?

34. Dermot MacMurrough

In pairs or with your teacher, read this story:

"It was a row between Tiernan O'Rourke, the one-eyed king of Briefne, and **Dermot MacMurrough**, King of Leinster, which made the Normans come to Ireland.

One night in 1152 Dermot kidnapped Tiernan's wife, Dervorgilla, along with a herd of cattle from Tiernan's kingdom. Dermot thundered off, back to his own kingdom.

Naturally, Tiernan was angry but he had to wait fourteen years for revenge on Dermot, because Dermot had powerful friends. Indeed one of these friends was the King of Tyrone, who was the High King at that time.

But after the King of Tyrone was killed in battle, Tiernan got the chance he had been waiting a long time for. Along with the King of Meath, who also hated Dermot, he took a large army and invaded Dermot's Kingdom of Leinster.

Dermot's castle was destroyed, but instead of making a last brave stand against his enemies, he fled to England with his daughter Aoife (pronounced *Eefa*), to try to get help from the Norman king who, at that time, was Henry II."

!

Now close the book and tell this story in your own words.

35. Dermot and the Normans

Dermot had been driven out of his kingdom and had run off to Henry II for help to get his land back. Now read this play. It tells the rest of the story.

Story-teller: After three days, Dermot and his daughter Aoife, and some of his men, reached Bristol, in England. Henry II was in France so they travelled on to France to meet him.

Henry II: Who did you say was out there? Speak up, man!

Servant: He says his name is Dare ... Dare ...

Henry II: Dare who?

Servant: He's from Ireland, my Lord, and he has a funny name ... Daremad.

Henry II: You're mad! Send him in. *(Dermot come in and bows low)* Welcome. What brings you here?

Dermot: Your Majesty, I have been wrongfully driven out of my kingdom of Leinster in Ireland. I beg your help to win it back. In return, I will swear loyalty to you. Ireland is a rich and fertile country. You and your lords could have great estates there.

Henry II (crossly): I know the Pope wants me to take over your unholy country, but I am far too busy to leave France.

Dermot: Perhaps, my Lord, you could send some of your men.

Henry II: All right, Dermot. I will give you a letter telling anyone who wishes to go that they have my permission. Take it to my lords in Wales. You will find plenty there willing to go to get land.

Dermot: Thank you, noble king — I will not forget this bargain.

Story-teller: Dermot sets off for Wales with the letter from Henry II. In Wales, Dermot and Aoife met a Norman lord called Richard de Clare. His nickname was **Strongbow.**

Strongbow: I will come to Ireland to help you, if you will let me marry your daughter and if you promise that one day I will be king of Leinster.

Dermot: Leinster has some of the finest land in Ireland. You will find that it is well worth your while coming to help me get my kingdom back.

Story-teller: Dermot set off home with some Norman soldiers to protect him. Other Norman armies arrived and soon Dermot had won his kingdom back. In 1170 Strongbow arrived and captured Waterford. He married Aoife.

Strongbow: Waterford is ours. Aoife and I will be married today. Soon we will march to Dublin and all Leinster will be ours.

!

Take turns to be each of the characters and act out this play in class.

Henry was cross when he told Dermot he was too busy to help him. Think about how each of the people speaking would have felt as they spoke.

Why do you think Richard de Clare got the nickname 'Strongbow'?

51

36. A wedding in Waterford

This is part of a famous painting which shows the wedding of Strongbow and Aoife.

?

Strongbow thought that just by marrying Aoife he would become King of Leinster. Why was this not true?

Marriage was an important way for great families to make agreements. As part of his agreement with the Normans, Dermot had promised that his daughter, Aoife, would marry Strongbow.

He also promised Strongbow the Kingdom of Leinster when he died.

The wedding of Strongbow and Aoife took place after Strongbow had fought with the Irish in Waterford in May 1170.

The writer, Morgan Llywelyn, wrote a book called *Strongbow*. This book told the story of Strongbow and Aoife. Here is a short piece from it:

"Your father is a clever man, Aoife. I hope I will be as good a king of Leinster one day." said Strongbow.

"You ...? King of Leinster? What makes you think you could ever be King of Leinster?" I asked in astonishment.

It was his turn to be astonished.

"Don't you know? Under feudal law, by marrying you I become your father's heir."

I was staring at him. "Don't you know? Under Irish law — and you're in Ireland now — no man can get a kingdom through a woman, be it mother or wife."

"Dermot lied to me!" cried Richard in a fury. Now I saw his eyes flash with lightening. Now I saw Strongbow, who could freeze his enemies blood with a glance.

37. Why the Normans came

So, as you have already seen, King Henry was too busy to come to Ireland himself, but some of his Norman lords in Wales came instead, to help Dermot. When the weather was very fine, the Welsh people could see Ireland from across the sea, and they knew that there was good land there.

Now, they had been invited to go to Ireland by one of its kings and, not only that, but their own king, Henry II, had given them permission to go. They promised to support Dermot, and he in turn promised them gold and silver and land.

He promised Strongbow that he could marry Aoife, his daughter, and that he could be King of Leinster after him. Although this was not usual under Irish law, Strongbow did become the next king.

?

1 Why do you think the Normans supported Dermot?

2 Read what Gerald of Wales said about the Irish. Would anything he said make the Normans want to come to Ireland?

3 Look at the map of Ulster. What do you think is the "big lake full of fish" that Gerald of Wales talked about?

Gerald of Wales wrote an account of the Irish at this time. Here are some of the things which he said about them:

- The Irish were unchristian
- They didn't marry or pay taxes
- When they gave their word they didn't keep it
- They were very musical
- They lived like animals
- There was a very big lake full of fish in Ulster

38. The Normans invade

At this time, the Irish were well used to being invaded. Over the centuries before this, the Vikings had invaded Ireland. They had raided and burnt monasteries and towns. Some of the Vikings had stayed in Ireland and settled near the coast or near rivers. Dublin was settled by the Vikings.

So when the Irish saw the Normans arriving in their open ships, speaking a foreign language and dressed for battle, it must have seemed like another Viking raid. Like the Vikings, the Normans rowed boats which had large sails and they hung their shields along the side of the boat.

The first Norman army arrived in Wexford in May 1169. Strongbow's army arrived in May 1170 and the third one arrived in September 1170.

The picture below shows a Norman ship from the Bayeux Tapestry.

Many monasteries had large **High Crosses**. Some of them have survived until today like this one at Clonmacnoise in Co Offaly. It is thirteen feet high.

39. The conquest of Ulster

This life-sized model of John de Courcy is at Carrickfergus Castle. He rides into the castle and a pageboy runs over to take his horse.

Many of the Normans who came to Ireland were very successful. Some of them built great castles and monasteries. They became so powerful that they began to think of themselves as kings.

This was a huge mistake. When you read about the feudal system, you learnt that the king was the most powerful person in the country and he would not want other men setting themselves up as kings.

One of these men was **John de Courcy**. He invaded Ulster in **1177**. It seems that Henry II had said that de Courcy could have Ulster if he could conquer it. Maybe Henry was only joking, but de Courcy took him seriously.

Gerald of Wales wrote this about John de Courcy:

"Only someone who was there and saw the blows dealt out by John de Courcy's sword, how it cut off now a head from someone's shoulders, or again arms or hand from their body, could properly praise the power of this great warrior."

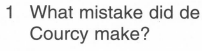

1 What mistake did de Courcy make?

2 Do you think Gerald of Wales was afraid of de Courcy? Say why.

40. De Courcy: the Norman who wanted to be king

Here is Affreca, sitting at a window in Carrickfergus Castle. Perhaps she is homesick and thinking of her family in the Isle of Man.

John de Courcy had fought bravely for Henry II in Ireland, but Henry had given him no reward. De Courcy knew that Ulster had not been captured yet.

In **1177**, de Courcy invaded Ulster with 22 knights and 300 soldiers. This was quite a small army. De Courcy knew that there was a story told by St Columba which said that Down would be captured by a small army. He wanted the people to feel that his was this army and so they would not fight so hard.

When de Courcy captured Down, he renamed it **Downpatrick** after the patron saint of Ireland. This was to make the people feel better about him.

To make up for fighting with the people, de Courcy built a monastery at Inch, near Downpatrick. He married Affreca, the daughter of the king of the Isle of Man. She set up a monastery at Greyabbey.

King John became king in 1199. He was jealous of de Courcy because he was so powerful, and sent another Norman lord in Ireland, **Hugh de Lacy**, to invade Ulster. De Lacy defeated de Courcy in **1205**.

After ruling Ulster for 27 years, de Courcy fled abroad and was poor for the rest of his life.

This is an artist's idea of what Grey Abbey would have looked like when it was built.

41. De Courcy's legacy lives on

After de Courcy captured Ulster, he got his followers to come and live there. The names Savage and Fitzsimmons became very common in the east of County Down and other parts of Ulster.

At least 80 mottes were built in Co Down and de Courcy created barons. He became too powerful and the king was afraid that he was setting himself up as a king in Ulster.

In 1205 King John gave de Courcy's lands to Hugh de Lacy.

This shop is in Carlingford, Co Louth. 'Savage' is a Norman surname.

It is said that families with these names settled in Ulster at this time:

Savage	Copeland
Chamberlain	Crolly
Jordan	Riddell
Russell	Mandeville
Fitzsimmons	Logan
White	Martell
Stokes	Benson
Stanton	Audley

!

Using a telephone directory, see how many families with the names Savage and Fitzsimmons (or Fitzsimons) still exist today.

Key Word: motte.

42. Carrickfergus Castle

This is the flag of John de Courcy who built Carrickfergus Castle in 1177.

Nowadays, when builders build houses, they dig foundations deep into the ground to give the walls a firm base so that they will not fall down.

Carrickfergus Castle has no foundations. It was built on rock using stone from the countryside around.

The keep has walls which are nine feet (270 cms) thick. The weight of these makes sure that they don't fall over.

The castle was built by John de Courcy in **1177**. However, over the next few decades, the flags and standards of three Norman families were to fly over Carrickfergus.

Key Word: foundations, decades.

?

Look at the picture of Carrickfergus Castle.

1 Do you think it was a strong castle?

2 Where would the safest place in the castle be?

Here are two life-size models in Carrickfergus Castle. On the left is a crossbow man and on the right is an archer. They are defending the castle against attack.

In 1205, **Hugh de Lacy** was ordered by the King to drive de Courcy out of Carrickfergus. The King felt that de Courcy had become too powerful as he had set himself up as the master of Ulster. He had even minted his own coins.

De Lacy was granted Carrickfergus Castle and was given the title **Earl of Ulster**.

It wasn't long before King John decided that de Lacy was getting too powerful. This time he came to Ireland himself to take Carrickfergus Castle. With a large army and many weapons, he besieged the castle for 9 days until it surrendered.

This is the flag of Hugh de Lacy.

This is the flag of King John.

44. *Carrickfergus Castle — change over time*

John de Courcy, Hugh de Lacy and King John all added bits to the castle.

The drawings below show how the castle changed over time.

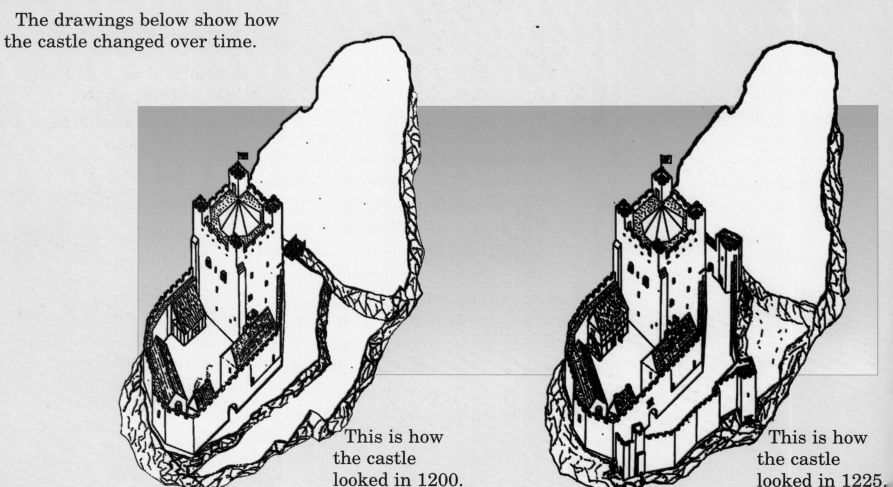

This is how the castle looked in 1200.

This is how the castle looked in 1225.

This is how the castle looked in 1250.

1   Study the drawings of Carrickfergus Castle.

Now decide if the statements below are true or false.

(a) A new wall was built by 1225. True or false?

(b) A second keep was added by 1225. True or false?

(c) The castle was bigger in 1250. True or false?

(d) More walls were built between 1225 and 1250. True or false?

2   Draw the flag of the Normans who ruled Carrickfergus Castle. Draw them in chronological order.

45. Norman soldiers and Irish soldiers

It is easy to think of the Normans as much better soldiers than the Irish. Even though the Normans won many battles in Ireland, sometimes this was because of the division between Irish kings rather than because the Normans were better fighters.

Sometimes even great soldiers like Strongbow were beaten in battle. For example, in 1173, he was trying to capture Kilkenny, but had to give up without success.

Strongbow never fought without Irish troops on his side and even John de Courcy conquered Ulster with Irish troops.

You read on page 53 some of the things which the medieval writer Gerald of Wales wrote about the Irish. Remember that Gerald was a Norman. He showed the Norman soldier as much better than the Irish soldier.

Here is an Irish soldier dressed for battle.

? Why do you think that Gerald tried to show that the Norman soldiers were better than the Irish soldiers? Pick one of these reasons:

1 The Norman soldiers *were* better.

2 He wanted to show the Irish as a backward people who deserved to be conquered.

3 He wanted to encourage Norman soldiers to come to Ireland as it would be easy to win land there.

VITA VERITAS VICTORIA

Many Norman families became rich and powerful. **Richard de Burgh** built his castle in Greencastle, Co Donegal, in 1305. Because of the colour of his hair he was nicknamed the Red Earl of Ulster.

There was a quarrel in the family and Richard's cousin, Walter, was put in prison in the castle at Greencastle. The story goes that he was starved to death in 1332. Walter had once saved the Earl's sister from drowning, so she tried to bring him food. But she was found out and thrown over the castle walls and killed.

Many years later, it is said that a skeleton was found chained to the walls of the castle keep. It is said to be this skeleton which is on Derry's coat of arms today. The words on the banner under the shield mean "Life, Truth, Victory".

Whatever the truth of the story, the Earl did not live very long after this. A year later he was stabbed to death in Carrickfergus, at the age of 21.

No one ever lived in the castle at Greencastle again.

?

Do you think this story is true?

Why would people make it up?

Close the classroom curtains and tell this story to the class. You can add bits to the story if you like.

You could also light a candle and listen to the story by candlelight.

1035 **William** becomes Duke of Normandy

1064 **Harold**, Earl of Godwin is shipwrecked and rescued by William.
Harold swears an oath to support William as the next King of England.

1066 Edward, King of England dies.
Harold is crowned king.
October 1st: William the Conqueror lands in England with an army.
October 14th: Harold and William fight the **Battle of Hastings**.
December 25th: **William is crowned King of England.**

1086 William carries out a survey of his kingdom. It is written in the **Domesday Book**.

1152 Dermot kidnaps Dervorgilla, wife of Tiernan, the king of Briefne.

1166 **Dermot MacMurrough** loses his kingdom of Leinster.
He goes to ask Henry II for help.

1169 *May 1st:* First Norman army arrives in Ireland.

1170 **Strongbow** arrives in Ireland with a Norman army.
He marries Aoife, the daughter of Dermot MacMurrough.

1177 **John de Courcy** invades Ulster.
He builds **Carrickfergus Castle**.

1205 **Hugh de Lacy** defeats John de Courcy.

1349 The **Black Death** sweeps across Europe and comes to Britain.